DO IT LATER!

A 2017 Planner (or Non-Planner)
for the
Creative Procrastinator

by Mark Asher

Pomegranate
PORTLAND, OREGON

Item No. U038

Pomegranate Communications, Inc.
19018 NE Portal Way, Portland OR 97230

Available in the United Kingdom and mainland Europe from Pomegranate Europe Ltd.
Unit 1, Heathcote Business Centre, Hurlbutt Road, Warwick, Warwickshire CV34 6TD, UK

Pomegranate publishes a wide variety of wall, mini wall, and desk calendars. Our extensive
line of paper gift products and books can be found at retail stores worldwide and online.
For more information or to place an order, please contact
Pomegranate Communications, Inc., 800 227 1428, www.pomegranate.com.

Designed by Patrice Morris

Dates in color indicate US federal holidays.
Dates listed for all astronomical events in this calendar are based on Coordinated Universal Time (UTC),
the worldwide system of civil timekeeping. UTC is essentially equivalent to Greenwich Mean Time.
Moon phases and US, Canadian, and UK holidays are noted.
Jewish and Islamic holidays begin at sunset on the day preceding the date listed.
Dates of Islamic holidays are given for North America and are subject to adjustment.

● NEW MOON   ◑ FIRST QUARTER   ○ FULL MOON   ◐ LAST QUARTER

Welcome, Procrastinator!

If due dates give you hives and you think efficiency is a dirty word, you've come to the right place. We procrastinators know the value of easing into the workday, of letting go of deadline pressure, of putting off distasteful tasks . . . until . . . it's . . . too late.

Do It Later! is designed for the way we time-indifferent people work. We're procrastinators—we get the important stuff done . . . when we get around to it. To be productive and creative, we first need to engage in critical activities, such as organizing our organizational strategies, staring out the window, creating the perfect playlist, and refilling our coffee. If you specialize in such delay tactics, or know someone who does, take a leisurely browse through the tips, activities, and wisdom sprinkled throughout this planner—for instance: "Deadlines are not living, breathing things—therefore, they can be buried, hidden, or forgotten" or "Having a task makes you feel alive and worthy. Why would you want to finish it quickly and feel empty?"

Then, start by writing a to-do item in a section that makes sense, such as "Things I have to do but that can wait a day, or two, or three . . . "; or "Small things I have to do before I can do the big things I have to do"; or "Things I absolutely have to do unless I absolutely don't want to do them." *Do It Later!* is filled with useful lists, such as "What You Can Do with a Small Window of Time" and "How to Take a Vacation without Leaving Your Office."

There's even a place to keep track of due dates and grace periods for your bills, a space to plan those crucial tax extensions, room to list contact information for procrastination partners, and weekly doodle blocks for that most beloved procrastination pastime.

Carry your new planner with pride. And if you never get around to starting the tasks you put in it—or even reading past this page—there's always tomorrow, or the day after, or . . .

—Mark Asher, fellow procrastinator

Procrastinator Wisdom

There is nothing like the satisfaction of doing nothing.

Things I have to do but that can wait a day, or two, or three . . .

Small things I have to do before I can do the big things I have to do

Things I absolutely have to do unless I absolutely don't want to do them

Things people have been bugging me to do for a really long time

CHRISTMAS HOLIDAY
BOXING DAY (CANADA, UK)
KWANZAA BEGINS

monday

26 361

CHRISTMAS HOLIDAY (CANADA, UK)

tuesday

27 362

wednesday

28 363

thursday

● **29** 364

friday

30 365

saturday

31 366

january

s	m	t	w	t	f	s
1	2	3	4	5	6	7
8	9	10	11	12	13	14
15	16	17	18	19	20	21
22	23	24	25	26	27	28
29	30	31				

NEW YEAR'S DAY

sunday

1 1

Procrastinator Tip

Scary things become less intimidating with repeat exposure. That's why I suggest looking at your workload several times before approaching it.

Things I have to do but that can wait a day, or two, or three . . .

Small things I have to do before I can do the big things I have to do

Things I absolutely have to do unless I absolutely don't want to do them

Things people have been bugging me to do for a really long time

doodle block

NEW YEAR'S DAY HOLIDAY

monday

2 2

BANK HOLIDAY (SCOTLAND)

tuesday

3 3

wednesday

4 4

thursday

◐ **5** 5

friday

6 6

saturday

7 7

sunday

8 8

january

s	m	t	w	t	f	s
1	2	3	4	5	6	7
8	9	10	11	12	13	14
15	16	17	18	19	20	21
22	23	24	25	26	27	28
29	30	31				

Procrastinator Wisdom

The reward for work is more work; the reward for leisure time is sweet memories.

Things I have to do but that can wait a day, or two, or three . . .

Small things I have to do before I can do the big things I have to do

Things I absolutely have to do unless I absolutely don't want to do them

Things people have been bugging me to do for a really long time

doodle block

monday

9 9

tuesday

10 10

wednesday

11 11

thursday

○ **12** 12

friday

13 13

saturday

14 14

sunday

15 15

january

s	m	t	w	t	f	s
1	2	3	4	5	6	7
8	9	10	11	12	13	14
15	16	17	18	19	20	21
22	23	24	25	26	27	28
29	30	31				

Procrastinator Activity

Make a comment on a provocative article online. This can lead to hours, if not days, of time-consuming conversation.

Things I have to do but that can wait a day, or two, or three . . .

Small things I have to do before I can do the big things I have to do

Things I absolutely have to do unless I absolutely don't want to do them

Things people have been bugging me to do for a really long time

doodle block

Email Lisa—
Wall—PDD
Re TT shift

Job procuring - Am.

TT shift 4-5
CG-Am

LT meeting @ 1:00pm.

Job procuring-Am

AHB - pm

K&L Res Weekend

january

s	m	t	w	t	f	s
1	2	3	4	5	6	7
8	9	10	11	12	13	14
15	16	17	18	19	20	21
22	23	24	25	26	27	28
29	30	31				

Procrastinator Tip

Postponement is the first step in acknowledging that something at hand eventually needs to get done.

Things I have to do but that can wait a day, or two, or three . . .

Small things I have to do before I can do the big things I have to do

Things I absolutely have to do unless I absolutely don't want to do them

Things people have been bugging me to do for a really long time

monday
23 23

CG-am

LT-pm

tuesday
24 24

Jason - 9-10   Erik 1030-12
Kenny - 1-2

wednesday
25 25

CG-Am

LT-pm

thursday
26 26

Job procuring - Am

Ryan. pm (Razor.).

friday
27 27

LUNAR NEW YEAR

saturday
● **28** 28

january

s	m	t	w	t	f	s
1	2	3	4	5	6	7
8	9	10	11	12	13	14
15	16	17	18	19	20	21
22	23	24	25	26	27	28
29	30	31				

sunday
29 29

Stuck in a Rut? Change Your Work Environment

1. Set up a tiny desk in front of a subway station bench. Don't hesitate to get input on your work from commuters.

2. Stake out the corner of a bookstore and grab two chairs—one to sit on and the other to use as a desk. If possible, situate yourself near the coffee counter.

3. Pack your work into a backpack and find a spot outdoors with inspiring views of nature.

4. Put a gigantic beanbag chair in your closet and take advantage of the comfort and quiet.

5. Work in your car overlooking a pleasant pasture filled with wildflowers, horses, and cows.

6. Sit in the lobby of a hospital for part of your day and realize how lucky you are to be able to work.

7. Run a hot bath and put a wooden board horizontally across it for your desk. Use the rim of the tub for your coffee cup, sticky notes, and other office supplies.

8. Sit cross-legged in front of your favorite painting at an art museum and draw inspiration.

List 10 things you hope will happen in the next 10 years.

1. _____

2. _____

3. _____

4. _____

5. _____

6. _____

7. _____

8. _____

9. _____

10. _____

Procrastinator Wisdom

The experts say procrastinators lack self-discipline, but I'm extremely disciplined when it comes to choosing to do something pleasurable rather than something painful.

Things I have to do but that can wait a day, or two, or three . . .

Small things I have to do before I can do the big things I have to do

Things I absolutely have to do unless I absolutely don't want to do them

Things people have been bugging me to do for a really long time

doodle block

CG.

LT

monday

30 30

CG =

MV @ Noon

tuesday

31 31

TT - Take Goals

Job Procurring - SN

LT   ESS MEETING

wednesday

1 32

TT - funding

Job Procurring -

Job Procurring - SN .

thursday

2 33

friday

3 34

saturday

◑ **4** 35

february

s	m	t	w	t	f	s
			1	2	3	4
5	6	7	8	9	10	11
12	13	14	15	16	17	18
19	20	21	22	23	24	25
26	27	28				

sunday

5 36

Procrastinator Tip

There's only one sure way to avoid Murphy's Law: don't plan anything!

Things I have to do but that can wait a day, or two, or three . . .

Small things I have to do before I can do the big things I have to do

Things I absolutely have to do unless I absolutely don't want to do them

Things people have been bugging me to do for a really long time

doodle block

CB—Invega @ 1:15 pm
Dr Edwards Meeting

LT - $60 grocery + $90 cheque

JL - 9-10   EO - 10:30-12

KS -1-2   ER - 2:30-3:30

Job Procurring .

LT -

Job Procurring - SN

Job Procurring-

february

s	m	t	w	t	f	s
			1	2	3	4
5	6	7	8	9	10	11
12	13	14	15	16	17	18
19	20	21	22	23	24	25
26	27	28				

Procrastinator Wisdom

They say procrastination is the thief of time. Well, if you can't save time or slow it down, you might as well steal it.

Things I have to do but that can wait a day, or two, or three . . .

Small things I have to do before I can do the big things I have to do

Things I absolutely have to do unless I absolutely don't want to do them

Things people have been bugging me to do for a really long time

doodle
block

February

---

monday

13 44

VALENTINE'S DAY   *tuesday*

14 45

---

wednesday

15 46

---

thursday

16 47

---

friday

17 48

---

saturday

◑ **18** 49

---

sunday

19 50

Procrastinator Activity

If, by some strange circumstance, you happen to have a to-do list already made, insert "Take a break" after every third item.

Things I have to do but that can wait a day, or two, or three . . .

Small things I have to do before I can do the big things I have to do

Things I absolutely have to do unless I absolutely don't want to do them

Things people have been bugging me to do for a really long time

doodle block

February

PRESIDENTS' DAY
FAMILY DAY (CANADA, SOME PROVINCES)

monday
20 51

tuesday
21 52

wednesday
22 53

thursday
23 54

friday
24 55

saturday
25 56

sunday
● 26 57

february

s	m	t	w	t	f	s
			1	2	3	4
5	6	7	8	9	10	11
12	13	14	15	16	17	18
19	20	21	22	23	24	25
26	27	28				

Procrastinator Wisdom

If I really wanted to I could probably beat procrastination, but I'm not a violent type.

Things I have to do but that can wait a day, or two, or three . . .

Small things I have to do before I can do the big things I have to do

Things I absolutely have to do unless I absolutely don't want to do them

Things people have been bugging me to do for a really long time

monday

27 58

MARDI GRAS

tuesday

28 59

ASH WEDNESDAY
ST. DAVID'S DAY (WALES)

wednesday

1 60

thursday

2 61

friday

3 62

saturday

4 63

march

s	m	t	w	t	f	s
			1	2	3	4
5	6	7	8	9	10	11
12	13	14	15	16	17	18
19	20	21	22	23	24	25
26	27	28	29	30	31	

sunday

◐ 5 64

The Underappreciated Upsides to Being a Procrastinator

1. By doing things at the last minute, time becomes more precious and meaningful.

2. Nobody trusts you with difficult or time-sensitive assignments.

3. You get the satisfaction of watching those eager-beaver types jump into new projects that you know horribly suck.

4. By setting the bar extremely low, you give your boss immense pleasure when you actually accomplish something.

5. You never miss breaking news and possess tons of trivial yet fascinating information.

6. By constantly performing under deadline pressure, your brain stays nimble.

7. Your back burner is frequently used and is never in need of repair.

Make a list of 10 things you can't afford but want to buy. Then read reviews online for each, until you're convinced that you have to have them.

1. _____

2. _____

3. _____

4. _____

5. _____

6. _____

7. _____

8. _____

9. _____

10. _____

Procrastinator Tip

The older you get, the harder it is to make new friends. That's why it's a good idea to spend lots of time on social media communicating with the friends you already have.

Things I have to do but that can wait a day, or two, or three . . .

Small things I have to do before I can do the big things I have to do

Things I absolutely have to do unless I absolutely don't want to do them

Things people have been bugging me to do for a really long time

March

monday

6 65

tuesday

7 66

INTERNATIONAL WOMEN'S DAY

wednesday

8 67

thursday

9 68

friday

10 69

saturday

11 70

march

s	m	t	w	t	f	s
			1	2	3	4
5	6	7	8	9	10	11
12	13	14	15	16	17	18
19	20	21	22	23	24	25
26	27	28	29	30	31	

PURIM

DAYLIGHT SAVING TIME BEGINS

sunday

○ **12** 71

Procrastinator Wisdom

How can procrastinating be acting against my own interests, when my interests are to stay in my pajamas, eat all day, and watch movies?

Things I have to do but that can wait a day, or two, or three . . .

Small things I have to do before I can do the big things I have to do

Things I absolutely have to do unless I absolutely don't want to do them

Things people have been bugging me to do for a really long time

March

monday

13 72

tuesday

14 73

wednesday

15 74

thursday

16 75

ST. PATRICK'S DAY
BANK HOLIDAY (N. IRELAND)

friday

17 76

saturday

18 77

march

s	m	t	w	t	f	s
			1	2	3	4
5	6	7	8	9	10	11
12	13	14	15	16	17	18
19	20	21	22	23	24	25
26	27	28	29	30	31	

sunday

19 78

Procrastinator Activity

Develop an elaborate 15-step process for refilling your coffee mug, complete with barista apron and espresso-machine sound effects.

Things I have to do but that can wait a day, or two, or three . . .

Small things I have to do before I can do the big things I have to do

Things I absolutely have to do unless I absolutely don't want to do them

Things people have been bugging me to do for a really long time

**doodle
block**

March

VERNAL EQUINOX 10:29 UTC

monday

◑ **20** 79

tuesday

21 80

wednesday

22 81

thursday

23 82

friday

24 83

saturday

25 84

march

s	m	t	w	t	f	s
			1	2	3	4
5	6	7	8	9	10	11
12	13	14	15	16	17	18
19	20	21	22	23	24	25
26	27	28	29	30	31	

MOTHERING SUNDAY (UK)
SUMMER TIME BEGINS (UK)

sunday

26 85

Procrastinator Wisdom

I can't help it if I excel at frivolous things.

Things I have to do but that can wait a day, or two, or three . . .

Small things I have to do before I can do the big things I have to do

Things I absolutely have to do unless I absolutely don't want to do them

Things people have been bugging me to do for a really long time

monday

27 86

tuesday

● **28** 87

wednesday

29 88

thursday

30 89

friday

31 90

saturday

1 91

sunday

2 92

april

s	m	t	w	t	f	s
						1
2	3	4	5	6	7	8
9	10	11	12	13	14	15
16	17	18	19	20	21	22
23	24	25	26	27	28	29
30						

Don't Tackle Tough Tasks
until You're Ready!

1. Complete all low-priority tasks first to clear your mind and establish a working rhythm.

2. Dim the lights to avoid glare and eyestrain. Put a pillow behind your head to avoid neck strain. Infuse your work space with soft music and candles to relax your mind.

3. Make sure your stomach is satiated. If you have to eat something first, be sure to wait half an hour before tackling any task.

4. Empty your trash can so that there is no distracting odor in the room.

5. Spend quality time on your favorite social media sites to solicit advice from fellow procrastinators on how to handle tough tasks.

6. Deactivate any software that might pop up and distract you.

7. Write a letter to yourself dated 10 days in advance praising the work you are about to do.

8. Set the alarm on your phone or watch to make sure you don't go at it for an extended period of time.

9. Have a long conversation with a friend beforehand so that you are talked out and ready to concentrate.

10. Arrange to have a coworker check on you an hour after you start working to offer encouragement and an energy bar.

Name 10 states that include the letter *t*.

1. _____

2. _____

3. _____

4. _____

5. _____

6. _____

7. _____

8. _____

9. _____

10. _____

Procrastinator Activity

Reorganize your to-do list on a smaller piece of paper, leaving off the items that don't fit.

Things I have to do but that can wait a day, or two, or three . . .

Small things I have to do before I can do the big things I have to do

Things I absolutely have to do unless I absolutely don't want to do them

Things people have been bugging me to do for a really long time

April

monday

◑ **3** 93

tuesday

4 94

wednesday

5 95

thursday

6 96

friday

7 97

saturday

8 98

april

s	m	t	w	t	f	s
						1
2	3	4	5	6	7	8
9	10	11	12	13	14	15
16	17	18	19	20	21	22
23	24	25	26	27	28	29
30						

PALM SUNDAY

sunday

9 99

Procrastinator Wisdom

Going through college without procrastinating is like swimming without getting wet—it's not practical or desirable.

Things I have to do but that can wait a day, or two, or three . . .

Small things I have to do before I can do the big things I have to do

Things I absolutely have to do unless I absolutely don't want to do them

Things people have been bugging me to do for a really long time

doodle
block

monday

10 100

PASSOVER BEGINS

tuesday

○ **11** 101

wednesday

12 102

thursday

13 103

GOOD FRIDAY
BANK HOLIDAY (CANADA, UK)

friday

14 104

saturday

15 105

EASTER

sunday

16 106

april

s	m	t	w	t	f	s
						1
2	3	4	5	6	7	8
9	10	11	12	13	14	15
16	17	18	19	20	21	22
23	24	25	26	27	28	29
30						

Procrastinator Tip

Surround yourself with enough doers and you'll never have to work a day in your life.

Things I have to do but that can wait a day, or two, or three . . .

Small things I have to do before I can do the big things I have to do

Things I absolutely have to do unless I absolutely don't want to do them

Things people have been bugging me to do for a really long time

April

EASTER MONDAY (CANADA, UK EXCEPT SCOTLAND)   *monday*

17 107

tuesday

18 108

wednesday

◑ **19** 109

thursday

20 110

friday

21 111

EARTH DAY   *saturday*

22 112

april

s	m	t	w	t	f	s
						1
2	3	4	5	6	7	8
9	10	11	12	13	14	15
16	17	18	19	20	21	22
23	24	25	26	27	28	29
30						

ST. GEORGE'S DAY (ENGLAND)   *sunday*

23 113

Procrastinator Activity

To stop procrastinating, first you need to know why you procrastinate. Think about this when you have some spare time.

Things I have to do but that can wait a day, or two, or three . . .

Small things I have to do before I can do the big things I have to do

Things I absolutely have to do unless I absolutely don't want to do them

Things people have been bugging me to do for a really long time

doodle
block

April

monday

24 114

tuesday

25 115

wednesday

● 26 116

thursday

27 117

friday

28 118

saturday

29 119

sunday

30 120

april

s	m	t	w	t	f	s
						1
2	3	4	5	6	7	8
9	10	11	12	13	14	15
16	17	18	19	20	21	22
23	24	25	26	27	28	29
30						

The Internet: The Procrastinator's Best Friend

1. I woke up on a Saturday fully intending to complete my household chores.

2. I vacuumed about half the living room when I became curious about the history of the vacuum cleaner, so I stopped to look it up online.

3. Did you know that before there were vacuum cleaners people used to take their carpets outside once a year to beat them clean?

4. I sat for a while longer, looking at photographs of the first vacuum cleaners ever made.

5. I eventually got back to the task at hand when my dog came in from the backyard. Like usual, he freaked out when he heard the roar of the vacuum.

6. I turned off the vacuum and wondered why dogs hate vacuum cleaners.

7. I stopped again to research it.

8. By the time I finished reading about ways to desensitize my dog to the vacuum cleaner—and to fireworks—I was ready for a nap.

Come up with 10 new nicknames to call your dog, cat, girlfriend/ boyfriend, or spouse.

1. _____

2. _____

3. _____

4. _____

5. _____

6. _____

7. _____

8. _____

9. _____

10. _____

Procrastinator Wisdom

Having a task makes you feel alive and worthy. Why would you want to finish it quickly and feel empty?

Things I have to do but that can wait a day, or two, or three . . .

Small things I have to do before I can do the big things I have to do

Things I absolutely have to do unless I absolutely don't want to do them

Things people have been bugging me to do for a really long time

doodle block

May

BANK HOLIDAY (UK)   *monday*

1 121

tuesday

2 122

wednesday

◐ **3** 123

thursday

4 124

CINCO DE MAYO   *friday*

5 125

saturday

6 126

sunday

7 127

may

s	m	t	w	t	f	s
	1	2	3	4	5	6
7	8	9	10	11	12	13
14	15	16	17	18	19	20
21	22	23	24	25	26	27
28	29	30	31			

Procrastinator Activity

When stress strikes, close your eyes and jot down the first 10 things you picture. Then write a short poem that includes these words.

Things I have to do but that can wait a day, or two, or three . . .

Small things I have to do before I can do the big things I have to do

Things I absolutely have to do unless I absolutely don't want to do them

Things people have been bugging me to do for a really long time

doodle
block

tuesday

9 129

wednesday

○ **10** 130

thursday

11 131

friday

12 132

saturday

13 133

may

s	m	t	w	t	f	s
	1	2	3	4	5	6
7	8	9	10	11	12	13
14	15	16	17	18	19	20
21	22	23	24	25	26	27
28	29	30	31			

MOTHER'S DAY

sunday

14 134

Procrastinator Wisdom

With so many days off for federal holidays, how about creating a government holiday for the people who loathe work the most—Procrastinators!

Things I have to do but that can wait a day, or two, or three . . .

Small things I have to do before I can do the big things I have to do

Things I absolutely have to do unless I absolutely don't want to do them

Things people have been bugging me to do for a really long time

monday

15 135

tuesday

16 136

wednesday

17 137

thursday

18 138

friday

◑ **19** 139

ARMED FORCES DAY

saturday

20 140

sunday

21 141

may

s	m	t	w	t	f	s
	1	2	3	4	5	6
7	8	9	10	11	12	13
14	15	16	17	18	19	20
21	22	23	24	25	26	27
28	29	30	31			

Procrastinator Tip

Good intentions are still good even if they're never acted upon.

Things I have to do but that can wait a day, or two, or three . . .

Small things I have to do before I can do the big things I have to do

Things I absolutely have to do unless I absolutely don't want to do them

Things people have been bugging me to do for a really long time

VICTORIA DAY (CANADA)

monday

22 142

tuesday

23 143

wednesday

24 144

thursday

● **25** 145

friday

26 146

RAMADAN BEGINS

saturday

27 147

sunday

28 148

may

s	m	t	w	t	f	s
	1	2	3	4	5	6
7	8	9	10	11	12	13
14	15	16	17	18	19	20
21	22	23	24	25	26	27
28	29	30	31			

How to Take a Vacation without Leaving Your Office

1. Do extensive research to determine your intended "destination." Check flight rates and times, weather conditions, and accommodations. Shop for new clothes if your "vacation" requires it.

2. Google your destination and print out large color photographs to adorn your office walls.

3. Send postcards to your coworkers to alert them of your upcoming, unique staycation.

4. Begin your vacation by playing sound cues that mimic your environment—crashing waves, screeching gulls, etc.

5. Put on suntan lotion every so often to trigger your olfactory system into believing you are anywhere but stuck in an office.

5. Create a daily itinerary, then close your eyes and imagine experiencing it.

6. Take virtual tours throughout the day via YouTube videos.

7. Have friends deliver "room service" to you, dressed for the part.

8. Create a photo album of your "trip" after it's over.

List 10 songs you never want to hear again and try to prevent them from replaying in your head as you make your list.

1. _____

2. _____

3. _____

4. _____

5. _____

6. _____

7. _____

8. _____

9. _____

10. _____

Procrastinator Wisdom

Hearing about the ills of procrastination is like reading the reasons not to skydive after you've left the plane.

Things I have to do but that can wait a day, or two, or three . . .

Small things I have to do before I can do the big things I have to do

Things I absolutely have to do unless I absolutely don't want to do them

Things people have been bugging me to do for a really long time

MEMORIAL DAY
BANK HOLIDAY (UK)

monday

29 149

tuesday

30 150

wednesday

31 151

thursday

◑ **1** 152

friday

2 153

saturday

3 154

sunday

4 155

june

s	m	t	w	t	f	s
				1	2	3
4	5	6	7	8	9	10
11	12	13	14	15	16	17
18	19	20	21	22	23	24
25	26	27	28	29	30	

Procrastinator Tip

In between sessions of procrastinating (or, if you must, working), it's important to take plenty of time to rest and eat right to enhance your recovery.

Things I have to do but that can wait a day, or two, or three . . .

Small things I have to do before I can do the big things I have to do

Things I absolutely have to do unless I absolutely don't want to do them

Things people have been bugging me to do for a really long time

doodle
block

monday

5 156

tuesday

6 157

wednesday

7 158

thursday

8 159

friday

○ **9** 160

saturday

10 161

sunday

11 162

june

s	m	t	w	t	f	s
				1	2	3
4	5	6	7	8	9	10
11	12	13	14	15	16	17
18	19	20	21	22	23	24
25	26	27	28	29	30	

Procrastinator Wisdom

My morning visualization led me through an incredibly productive work period, but I ended up visiting two museums and a national park, and having dessert with a friend by the time I opened my eyes.

Things I have to do but that can wait a day, or two, or three . . .

Small things I have to do before I can do the big things I have to do

Things I absolutely have to do unless I absolutely don't want to do them

Things people have been bugging me to do for a really long time

monday

12 163

tuesday

13 164

FLAG DAY

wednesday

14 165

thursday

15 166

friday

16 167

saturday

◑ **17** 168

FATHER'S DAY

sunday

18 169

june

s	m	t	w	t	f	s
				1	2	3
4	5	6	7	8	9	10
11	12	13	14	15	16	17
18	19	20	21	22	23	24
25	26	27	28	29	30	

Procrastinator Activity

Using only emojis, text elaborate murals to your friends.

Things I have to do but that can wait a day, or two, or three . . .

Small things I have to do before I can do the big things I have to do

Things I absolutely have to do unless I absolutely don't want to do them

Things people have been bugging me to do for a really long time

June

monday

19 170

tuesday

20 171

SUMMER SOLSTICE 04:24 UTC

wednesday

21 172

thursday

22 173

friday

23 174

saturday

● **24** 175

EID AL-FITR

sunday

25 176

june

s	m	t	w	t	f	s
				1	2	3
4	5	6	7	8	9	10
11	12	13	14	15	16	17
18	19	20	21	22	23	24
25	26	27	28	29	30	

Procrastinator Wisdom

With deadlines looming, a thought like this will enter my head: can one procrastinate without being a procrastinator?

Things I have to do but that can wait a day, or two, or three . . .

Small things I have to do before I can do the big things I have to do

Things I absolutely have to do unless I absolutely don't want to do them

Things people have been bugging me to do for a really long time

doodle block

monday

26 177

tuesday

27 178

wednesday

28 179

thursday

29 180

friday

30 181

CANADA DAY (CANADA)

saturday

◑ **1** 182

sunday

2 183

july

s	m	t	w	t	f	s
						1
2	3	4	5	6	7	8
9	10	11	12	13	14	15
16	17	18	19	20	21	22
23	24	25	26	27	28	29
30	31					

Procrastination with a Purpose

1. Empty the contents of all of your storage boxes. Take inventory on each item to create a master storage list. Then go buy different colored boxes that reflect the mood of each box's contents.

2. Make a shrine of your work on your office walls that will impress your boss and coworkers.

3. Take inventory of all your office supplies. Visit office supply websites and compare prices of the items you use. Then blog about your findings and what you miss most about old-fashioned stationery stores.

4. Buy three different laundry detergents and do a smell test on which one is the best.

5. Tour every coffee joint in town and sample different brews. After coffee tasting, visit a mattress store to see which mattress gives you the best chance for sleep in an overly caffeinated state.

6. Purchase dispensers for your soap, shampoo, lotion, shaving cream, and anything else that is liquid. Create funky, fun labels for each.

7. Memorize which stores and restaurants are open during major holidays.

8. Spend an entire summer day watching how the sun revolves around your home. Then visit a home improvement center to explore your inside and outside shading options.

If you had to choose only 10 foods to eat for the rest of your life, what would they be?

1. _____

2. _____

3. _____

4. _____

5. _____

6. _____

7. _____

8. _____

9. _____

10. _____

Procrastinator Tip

Deadlines are not living, breathing things—therefore, they can be buried, hidden, or forgotten.

Things I have to do but that can wait a day, or two, or three . . .

Small things I have to do before I can do the big things I have to do

Things I absolutely have to do unless I absolutely don't want to do them

Things people have been bugging me to do for a really long time

doodle block

monday

3 184

INDEPENDENCE DAY   *tuesday*

4 185

wednesday

5 186

thursday

6 187

friday

7 188

saturday

8 189

sunday

○ **9** 190

july

s	m	t	w	t	f	s
						1
2	3	4	5	6	7	8
9	10	11	12	13	14	15
16	17	18	19	20	21	22
23	24	25	26	27	28	29
30	31					

Procrastinator Activity

Pick two completely unrelated topics, such as retirement planning and cauliflower. Start a Google search for one topic, then attempt to navigate to the other topic by clicking on links.

Things I have to do but that can wait a day, or two, or three . . .

Small things I have to do before I can do the big things I have to do

Things I absolutely have to do unless I absolutely don't want to do them

Things people have been bugging me to do for a really long time

doodle block

10 191

tuesday

11 192

BATTLE OF THE BOYNE (N. IRELAND) *wednesday*

12 193

thursday

13 194

friday

14 195

saturday

15 196

july

s	m	t	w	t	f	s
						1
2	3	4	5	6	7	8
9	10	11	12	13	14	15
16	17	18	19	20	21	22
23	24	25	26	27	28	29
30	31					

sunday

◐ **16** 197

Procrastinator Wisdom

It's true—procrastination doesn't pay. But who said I was *expecting* something for doing nothing?

Things I have to do but that can wait a day, or two, or three . . .

Small things I have to do before I can do the big things I have to do

Things I absolutely have to do unless I absolutely don't want to do them

Things people have been bugging me to do for a really long time

doodle block

monday

17 198

tuesday

18 199

wednesday

19 200

thursday

20 201

friday

21 202

saturday

22 203

sunday

● **23** 204

july

s	m	t	w	t	f	s
						1
2	3	4	5	6	7	8
9	10	11	12	13	14	15
16	17	18	19	20	21	22
23	24	25	26	27	28	29
30	31					

Procrastinator Tip

The experts and I agree: tackle small tasks first. Here's where we disagree: they believe this builds confidence and leads to the next item on your to-do list; I think it calls for a snack break or a nap.

Things I have to do but that can wait a day, or two, or three . . .

Small things I have to do before I can do the big things I have to do

Things I absolutely have to do unless I absolutely don't want to do them

Things people have been bugging me to do for a really long time

doodle
block

monday

24 205

tuesday

25 206

wednesday

26 207

thursday

27 208

friday

28 209

saturday

29 210

sunday

◐ **30** 211

july

s	m	t	w	t	f	s
						1
2	3	4	5	6	7	8
9	10	11	12	13	14	15
16	17	18	19	20	21	22
23	24	25	26	27	28	29
30	31					

What You Can Do with a Small Window of Time

1. Clean it to relieve your stress and improve your view.

2. Open it so you can get some fresh air and think clearly.

3. Use a washable window marker to write what you hope to accomplish within your limited time.

4. Write a poem or a song about your small window of time.

5. Pray for a larger window of time.

6. Make an expanded to-do list in the event that your prayer is answered.

7. Ask people in your office to define a "window of time."

8. Complain to your boss that your small window of time doesn't let in enough light and makes your workspace feel cramped.

List 10 reasons you deserve a raise.

1. _____

2. _____

3. _____

4. _____

5. _____

6. _____

7. _____

8. _____

9. _____

10. _____

Procrastinator Activity

Register for the longest antiprocrastination seminar you can find. Bonus if it's during an especially busy time at work.

Things I have to do but that can wait a day, or two, or three . . .

Small things I have to do before I can do the big things I have to do

Things I absolutely have to do unless I absolutely don't want to do them

Things people have been bugging me to do for a really long time

Jul / Aug

monday

31 212

tuesday

1 213

wednesday

2 214

thursday

3 215

friday

4 216

saturday

5 217

sunday

6 218

august

s	m	t	w	t	f	s
			1	2	3	4	5
6	7	8	9	10	11	12
13	14	15	16	17	18	19
20	21	22	23	24	25	26
27	28	29	30	31		

Procrastinator Wisdom

If there is no time like the present, why would I want to spend it working?

Things I have to do but that can wait a day, or two, or three . . .

Small things I have to do before I can do the big things I have to do

Things I absolutely have to do unless I absolutely don't want to do them

Things people have been bugging me to do for a really long time

August

CIVIC HOLIDAY (CANADA, MOST PROVINCES)
BANK HOLIDAY (SCOTLAND)

monday

○ **7** 219

tuesday

8 220

wednesday

9 221

thursday

10 222

friday

11 223

saturday

12 224

sunday

13 225

august

s	m	t	w	t	f	s
		1	2	3	4	5
6	7	8	9	10	11	12
13	14	15	16	17	18	19
20	21	22	23	24	25	26
27	28	29	30	31		

Procrastinator Activity

Plan the reward for finishing your work and then try it out to make sure you like it.

Things I have to do but that can wait a day, or two, or three . . .

Small things I have to do before I can do the big things I have to do

Things I absolutely have to do unless I absolutely don't want to do them

Things people have been bugging me to do for a really long time

doodle
block

August

tuesday

◑ **15** 227

wednesday

16 228

thursday

17 229

friday

18 230

saturday

19 231

august

s	m	t	w	t	f	s
		1	2	3	4	5
6	7	8	9	10	11	12
13	14	15	16	17	18	19
20	21	22	23	24	25	26
27	28	29	30	31		

sunday

20 232

Procrastinator Wisdom

If good things come to those who wait, isn't it wise to make sure you don't act in haste?

Things I have to do but that can wait a day, or two, or three . . .

Small things I have to do before I can do the big things I have to do

Things I absolutely have to do unless I absolutely don't want to do them

Things people have been bugging me to do for a really long time

August

monday

● **21** 233

tuesday

22 234

wednesday

23 235

thursday

24 236

friday

25 237

saturday

26 238

sunday

27 239

august

s	m	t	w	t	f	s
		1	2	3	4	5
6	7	8	9	10	11	12
13	14	15	16	17	18	19
20	21	22	23	24	25	26
27	28	29	30	31		

Why People Procrastinate

1. Someone has to be a counterbalance to the maddening pace of modern culture and the increased demands it puts on people.

2. Avoiding something dreadful in favor of doing something enjoyable is simply common sense.

3. Procrastinators possess magical thinking—the belief that if something is delayed for long enough it will disappear.

4. Procrastinators understand that everything has a price and that a little bit of anxiety, guilt, and dread is a worthwhile cost for avoiding something you loathe.

5. It makes life more dramatic and exciting when you finally tackle a task at the 11th hour.

6. Procrastinators have an innate ability to spot the unpleasant aspects of life and have the courage and conviction to dance around them.

7. Procrastinators are wild optimists who believe that tomorrow is always better than today.

8. "Save the best for last" isn't just an old adage, it's a way of life.

List 10 fictional characters you would bring to life if you could.

1. _____

2. _____

3. _____

4. _____

5. _____

6. _____

7. _____

8. _____

9. _____

10. _____

Procrastinator Wisdom

Some people may call it procrastinating, but I call it waiting for all the information.

Things I have to do but that can wait a day, or two, or three . . .

Small things I have to do before I can do the big things I have to do

Things I absolutely have to do unless I absolutely don't want to do them

Things people have been bugging me to do for a really long time

BANK HOLIDAY (UK EXCEPT SCOTLAND)   *monday*

28 240

tuesday

◐ **29** 241

wednesday

30 242

thursday

31 243

EID AL-ADHA   *friday*

1 244

saturday

2 245

september

s	m	t	w	t	f	s
					1	2
3	4	5	6	7	8	9
10	11	12	13	14	15	16
17	18	19	20	21	22	23
24	25	26	27	28	29	30

sunday

3 246

Procrastinator Tip

Cyberslacking may be a serious deterrent to productivity, but it sure does pass the time quickly.

Things I have to do but that can wait a day, or two, or three . . .

Small things I have to do before I can do the big things I have to do

Things I absolutely have to do unless I absolutely don't want to do them

Things people have been bugging me to do for a really long time

doodle block

September

LABOR DAY (US, CANADA)   *monday*

4 247

tuesday

5 248

wednesday

○ 6 249

thursday

7 250

friday

8 251

saturday

9 252

september

s	m	t	w	t	f	s
					1	2
3	4	5	6	7	8	9
10	11	12	13	14	15	16
17	18	19	20	21	22	23
24	25	26	27	28	29	30

sunday

10 253

Procrastinator Wisdom

The moment you decide you're not going to do what you're supposed to do is called freedom.

Things I have to do but that can wait a day, or two, or three . . .

Small things I have to do before I can do the big things I have to do

Things I absolutely have to do unless I absolutely don't want to do them

Things people have been bugging me to do for a really long time

September

monday

11 ₂₅₄

tuesday

12 ₂₅₅

wednesday

◐ **13** ₂₅₆

thursday

14 ₂₅₇

friday

15 ₂₅₈

saturday

16 ₂₅₉

september

s	m	t	w	t	f	s
					1	2
3	4	5	6	7	8	9
10	11	12	13	14	15	16
17	18	19	20	21	22	23
24	25	26	27	28	29	30

sunday

17 ₂₆₀

Procrastinator Activity

My psychologist suggested that I time travel to a place in the future where I felt good about finishing a big project. Somehow I ended up on a beach with my feet in the sand and a drink in my hand.

Things I have to do but that can wait a day, or two, or three . . .

Small things I have to do before I can do the big things I have to do

Things I absolutely have to do unless I absolutely don't want to do them

Things people have been bugging me to do for a really long time

September

monday

18 261

tuesday

19 262

wednesday

● **20** 263

ROSH HASHANAH

MUHARRAM

INTERNATIONAL DAY OF PEACE

thursday

21 264

AUTUMNAL EQUINOX 20:02 UTC

friday

22 265

saturday

23 266

september

s	m	t	w	t	f	s
					1	2
3	4	5	6	7	8	9
10	11	12	13	14	15	16
17	18	19	20	21	22	23
24	25	26	27	28	29	30

sunday

24 267

Procrastinator Wisdom

To relax or to work, that is never the question.

Things I have to do but that can wait a day, or two, or three . . .

Small things I have to do before I can do the big things I have to do

Things I absolutely have to do unless I absolutely don't want to do them

Things people have been bugging me to do for a really long time

monday

25 268

tuesday

26 269

wednesday

27 270

thursday

◑ **28** 271

friday

29 272

YOM KIPPUR
ASHURA

saturday

30 273

sunday

1 274

october

s	m	t	w	t	f	s
1	2	3	4	5	6	7
8	9	10	11	12	13	14
15	16	17	18	19	20	21
22	23	24	25	26	27	28
29	30	31				

The Best Ways to Clear
a Cluttered Mind

1. Lie on your side and imagine all your worries, woes, and work deadlines draining out of your ear. Then roll over and do it on the other side. This will empty both left and right brains.

2. Make a paper airplane out of your to-do list and fly it off a tall bridge.

3. Leave your office and walk around a one-mile radius, stopping every 50 steps and sitting down for 10 minutes. If you happen to stop in front of a coffee shop or bar, so be it.

4. Close your door, turn on some New Age music, and do a headstand. If you can't manage that, try to touch your toes instead. Don't hurt yourself.

5. Throw darts (or anything else you would like) at an image of a clock.

6. Learn how to say "Work does not define me; therefore I am free" in 10 different languages.

7. Every time you think about work, sing the first song that pops into your head, unless it's "The Little Drummer Boy." (Oops, now that's in your head. Sorry.)

8. Let your mind go on a fantasy vacation and imagine what you'll order from room service.

9. Eat some cookies. Really. This works.

10. Watch a cloud until it dissipates or drifts away. Then write a haiku about it.

Make a list of 10 things you wish were included in your job description.

1. _____

2. _____

3. _____

4. _____

5. _____

6. _____

7. _____

8. _____

9. _____

10. _____

Procrastinator Tip

Research shows that humans are wired to procrastinate. Why mess with God's creation?

Things I have to do but that can wait a day, or two, or three . . .

Small things I have to do before I can do the big things I have to do

Things I absolutely have to do unless I absolutely don't want to do them

Things people have been bugging me to do for a really long time

October

monday

2 275

tuesday

3 276

wednesday

4 277

thursday

○ **5** 278

friday

6 279

saturday

7 280

sunday

8 281

october

s	m	t	w	t	f	s
1	2	3	4	5	6	7
8	9	10	11	12	13	14
15	16	17	18	19	20	21
22	23	24	25	26	27	28
29	30	31				

Procrastinator Wisdom

If they can come up with ways to cure procrastination, certainly they can come up with ways to do nothing and still make money.

Things I have to do but that can wait a day, or two, or three . . .

Small things I have to do before I can do the big things I have to do

Things I absolutely have to do unless I absolutely don't want to do them

Things people have been bugging me to do for a really long time

doodle
block

COLUMBUS DAY
THANKSGIVING DAY (CANADA)

monday

9 282

tuesday

10 283

wednesday

11 284

thursday

◐ **12** 285

friday

13 286

saturday

14 287

sunday

15 288

october

s	m	t	w	t	f	s
1	2	3	4	5	6	7
8	9	10	11	12	13	14
15	16	17	18	19	20	21
22	23	24	25	26	27	28
29	30	31				

Procrastinator Activity

Type "procrastination cure" into Google. Go through the top 1,000 results and make a detailed list of cures to try someday.

Things I have to do but that can wait a day, or two, or three . . .

Small things I have to do before I can do the big things I have to do

Things I absolutely have to do unless I absolutely don't want to do them

Things people have been bugging me to do for a really long time

doodle
block

October

monday

16 289

tuesday

17 290

wednesday

18 291

thursday

● **19** 292

friday

20 293

saturday

21 294

october

s	m	t	w	t	f	s
1	2	3	4	5	6	7
8	9	10	11	12	13	14
15	16	17	18	19	20	21
22	23	24	25	26	27	28
29	30	31				

sunday

22 295

Procrastinator Wisdom

I subscribe to the theory of relativity—if I don't feel like doing something, I get one of my siblings to do it.

Things I have to do but that can wait a day, or two, or three . . .

Small things I have to do before I can do the big things I have to do

Things I absolutely have to do unless I absolutely don't want to do them

Things people have been bugging me to do for a really long time

October

monday

23 296

UNITED NATIONS DAY

tuesday

24 297

wednesday

25 298

thursday

26 299

friday

◖ **27** 300

saturday

28 301

october

s	m	t	w	t	f	s
	1	2	3	4	5	6	7
8	9	10	11	12	13	14
15	16	17	18	19	20	21
22	23	24	25	26	27	28
29	30	31				

SUMMER TIME ENDS (UK)

sunday

29 302

If You Absolutely Must Stop Procrastinating . . .

1. Tie your shoelaces to your desk so you can't wander off.

2. Make your own hourglass and fill it with honey instead of sand.

3. Cover your windows with tin foil. It'll block out the distractions and the heat and it'll make you look like a loser when you're staring at it instead of working.

4. Draw up a self-management contract that carries stiff penalties for not finishing your work.

5. Change the ring tone on your phone to say in a loud, obnoxious voice: "Don't you dare answer this call! Keep working!"

6. Treat yourself like a child and block all your favorite websites.

7. Hire a security guard to watch you work.

8. Make expensive wagers with your fellow employees that will cost you big time if you don't complete your work.

9. Put a webcam on your computer that has a live feed to your boss's office.

Think up 10 aliases you could use if you become rich and famous and need to travel incognito.

1. _____

2. _____

3. _____

4. _____

5. _____

6. _____

7. _____

8. _____

9. _____

10. _____

Procrastinator Activity

If you break your most important task into chunks . . . then pieces . . . then morsels, you'll end up with a challenging jigsaw puzzle to work on.

Things I have to do but that can wait a day, or two, or three . . .

Small things I have to do before I can do the big things I have to do

Things I absolutely have to do unless I absolutely don't want to do them

Things people have been bugging me to do for a really long time

Oct / Nov

monday

30 303

HALLOWEEN

tuesday

31 304

wednesday

1 305

thursday

2 306

friday

3 307

saturday

○ **4** 308

DAYLIGHT SAVING TIME ENDS

sunday

5 309

november

s	m	t	w	t	f	s
			1	2	3	4
5	6	7	8	9	10	11
12	13	14	15	16	17	18
19	20	21	22	23	24	25
26	27	28	29	30		

Procrastinator Tip

Wait until the last minute to do something. It should only take a minute to finish it.

Things I have to do but that can wait a day, or two, or three . . .

Small things I have to do before I can do the big things I have to do

Things I absolutely have to do unless I absolutely don't want to do them

Things people have been bugging me to do for a really long time

November

monday

6 310

tuesday

7 311

wednesday

8 312

thursday

9 313

VETERANS DAY HOLIDAY

friday

◑ **10** 314

VETERANS DAY
REMEMBRANCE DAY (CANADA)

saturday

11 315

REMEMBRANCE DAY (UK)

sunday

12 316

november

s	m	t	w	t	f	s
			1	2	3	4
5	6	7	8	9	10	11
12	13	14	15	16	17	18
19	20	21	22	23	24	25
26	27	28	29	30		

Procrastinator Wisdom

I don't want the time I wasted back, I want back the time I worked!

Things I have to do but that can wait a day, or two, or three . . .

Small things I have to do before I can do the big things I have to do

Things I absolutely have to do unless I absolutely don't want to do them

Things people have been bugging me to do for a really long time

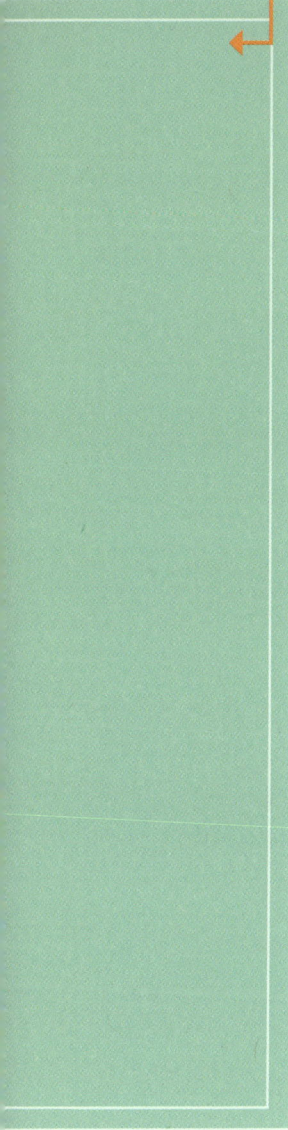

doodle block

November

monday

13 317

tuesday

14 318

wednesday

15 319

thursday

16 320

friday

17 321

saturday

● **18** 322

sunday

19 323

november

s	m	t	w	t	f	s
			1	2	3	4
5	6	7	8	9	10	11
12	13	14	15	16	17	18
19	20	21	22	23	24	25
26	27	28	29	30		

Procrastinator Tip

Learn to love your inner procrastinator. It makes a great accomplice for your inner child.

Things I have to do but that can wait a day, or two, or three . . .

Small things I have to do before I can do the big things I have to do

Things I absolutely have to do unless I absolutely don't want to do them

Things people have been bugging me to do for a really long time

doodle block

monday

20 324

tuesday

21 325

wednesday

22 326

THANKSGIVING DAY

thursday

23 327

friday

24 328

saturday

25 329

november

s	m	t	w	t	f	s
			1	2	3	4
5	6	7	8	9	10	11
12	13	14	15	16	17	18
19	20	21	22	23	24	25
26	27	28	29	30		

sunday

◗ **26** 330

What You Can Do with This Planner at the End of the Year

1. Use it as a drink coaster on New Year's Eve.

2. Give it to a fellow procrastinator who is a year behind.

3. Draw a bottle on the cover and play spin the bottle.

4. Use the pages to make a wall collage that spells out HELP.

5. Give it to your boss as a gag gift with a card that says, "This is how I made it through 2017!"

6. Open it halfway, turn it facedown, and use it as a tent for your computer's mouse.

7. Make an awesome fleet of paper airplanes with the colored pages.

8. Write one of these words—*Now, Later, or Never*—on each of the edges of the planner. Spin it whenever you're in doubt and follow the action that points toward you. If you get the spiral edge, *Delegate.*

Make a list of the 10 best meals you can make from peanut butter.

1. _____

2. _____

3. _____

4. _____

5. _____

6. _____

7. _____

8. _____

9. _____

10. _____

Procrastinator Wisdom

You can't stop time, but you can slow it down by savoring it.

Things I have to do but that can wait a day, or two, or three . . .

Small things I have to do before I can do the big things I have to do

Things I absolutely have to do unless I absolutely don't want to do them

Things people have been bugging me to do for a really long time

doodle
block

monday

27 331

tuesday

28 332

wednesday

29 333

ST. ANDREW'S DAY (SCOTLAND)   *thursday*

30 334

MAWLID AN-NABI   *friday*

1 335

saturday

2 336

sunday

○ **3** 337

december

s	m	t	w	t	f	s
					1	2
3	4	5	6	7	8	9
10	11	12	13	14	15	16
17	18	19	20	21	22	23
24	25	26	27	28	29	30
31						

Procrastinator Tip

Always include an expiration date beside each task on your to-do list.

Things I have to do but that can wait a day, or two, or three . . .

Small things I have to do before I can do the big things I have to do

Things I absolutely have to do unless I absolutely don't want to do them

Things people have been bugging me to do for a really long time

December

monday

4 338

tuesday

5 339

wednesday

6 340

thursday

7 341

friday

8 342

saturday

9 343

sunday

◐ **10** 344

december

s	m	t	w	t	f	s
					1	2
3	4	5	6	7	8	9
10	11	12	13	14	15	16
17	18	19	20	21	22	23
24	25	26	27	28	29	30
31						

Procrastinator Activity

Challenge yourself to join as many social media sites as possible in one workday. Create a supersecret spreadsheet of all their logins and passwords.

Things I have to do but that can wait a day, or two, or three . . .

Small things I have to do before I can do the big things I have to do

Things I absolutely have to do unless I absolutely don't want to do them

Things people have been bugging me to do for a really long time

December

monday

11 345

tuesday

12 346

HANUKKAH BEGINS   *wednesday*

13 347

thursday

14 348

friday

15 349

saturday

16 350

december

s	m	t	w	t	f	s
					1	2
3	4	5	6	7	8	9
10	11	12	13	14	15	16
17	18	19	20	21	22	23
24	25	26	27	28	29	30
31						

sunday

17 351

Procrastinator Wisdom

If absence makes the heart grow fonder, I should get up and leave my office right now!

Things I have to do but that can wait a day, or two, or three . . .

Small things I have to do before I can do the big things I have to do

Things I absolutely have to do unless I absolutely don't want to do them

Things people have been bugging me to do for a really long time

December

monday

● **18** 352

tuesday

19 353

wednesday

20 354

WINTER SOLSTICE 16:28 UTC

thursday

21 355

friday

22 356

saturday

23 357

december

s	m	t	w	t	f	s
					1	2
3	4	5	6	7	8	9
10	11	12	13	14	15	16
17	18	19	20	21	22	23
24	25	26	27	28	29	30
31						

sunday

24 358

Procrastinator Activity

If you open and close your refrigerator enough times, items will disappear.

Things I have to do but that can wait a day, or two, or three . . .

Small things I have to do before I can do the big things I have to do

Things I absolutely have to do unless I absolutely don't want to do them

Things people have been bugging me to do for a really long time

December

CHRISTMAS

monday

25 359

BOXING DAY (CANADA, UK)

KWANZAA BEGINS

tuesday

◑ **26** 360

wednesday

27 361

thursday

28 362

friday

29 363

saturday

30 364

sunday

31 365

Procrastinator Wisdom

Critics say being a productive procrastinator is sort of like being a rock that swims. They might have a point there.

Things I have to do but that can wait a day, or two, or three . . .

Small things I have to do before I can do the big things I have to do

Things I absolutely have to do unless I absolutely don't want to do them

Things people have been bugging me to do for a really long time

NEW YEAR'S DAY

monday

1 ₁

BANK HOLIDAY (SCOTLAND)

tuesday

○ **2** ₂

wednesday

3 ₃

thursday

4 ₄

friday

5 ₅

saturday

6 ₆

sunday

7 ₇

january

s	m	t	w	t	f	s
	1	2	3	4	5	6
7	8	9	10	11	12	13
14	15	16	17	18	19	20
21	22	23	24	25	26	27
28	29	30	31			

Grace Periods for Bills Due & Tax Extension Schedule/Plan

1. _____

2. _____

3. _____

4. _____

5. _____

6. _____

7. _____

8. _____

9. _____

10. _____

People to Call or Text
When You Don't Feel Like Working

NAME

MOBILE

PHONE (H)

PHONE (W)

NAME

MOBILE

PHONE (H)

PHONE (W)

NAME

MOBILE

PHONE (H)

PHONE (W)

NAME

MOBILE

PHONE (H)

PHONE (W)

2018

january

s	m	t	w	t	f	s
	1	2	3	4	5	6
7	8	9	10	11	12	13
14	15	16	17	18	19	20
21	22	23	24	25	26	27
28	29	30	31			

february

s	m	t	w	t	f	s
				1	2	3
4	5	6	7	8	9	10
11	12	13	14	15	16	17
18	19	20	21	22	23	24
25	26	27	28			

march

s	m	t	w	t	f	s
				1	2	3
4	5	6	7	8	9	10
11	12	13	14	15	16	17
18	19	20	21	22	23	24
25	26	27	28	29	30	31

april

s	m	t	w	t	f	s
1	2	3	4	5	6	7
8	9	10	11	12	13	14
15	16	17	18	19	20	21
22	23	24	25	26	27	28
29	30					

may

s	m	t	w	t	f	s
		1	2	3	4	5
6	7	8	9	10	11	12
13	14	15	16	17	18	19
20	21	22	23	24	25	26
27	28	29	30	31		

june

s	m	t	w	t	f	s
					1	2
3	4	5	6	7	8	9
10	11	12	13	14	15	16
17	18	19	20	21	22	23
24	25	26	27	28	29	30

july

s	m	t	w	t	f	s
1	2	3	4	5	6	7
8	9	10	11	12	13	14
15	16	17	18	19	20	21
22	23	24	25	26	27	28
29	30	31				

august

s	m	t	w	t	f	s
			1	2	3	4
5	6	7	8	9	10	11
12	13	14	15	16	17	18
19	20	21	22	23	24	25
26	27	28	29	30	31	

september

s	m	t	w	t	f	s
						1
2	3	4	5	6	7	8
9	10	11	12	13	14	15
16	17	18	19	20	21	22
23	24	25	26	27	28	29
30						

october

s	m	t	w	t	f	s
	1	2	3	4	5	6
7	8	9	10	11	12	13
14	15	16	17	18	19	20
21	22	23	24	25	26	27
28	29	30	31			

november

s	m	t	w	t	f	s
				1	2	3
4	5	6	7	8	9	10
11	12	13	14	15	16	17
18	19	20	21	22	23	24
25	26	27	28	29	30	

december

s	m	t	w	t	f	s
						1
2	3	4	5	6	7	8
9	10	11	12	13	14	15
16	17	18	19	20	21	22
23	24	25	26	27	28	29
30	31					